Florida

Facts and Symbols

by Emily McAuliffe

Consultant:
Michael Ross Odom
Social Studies Curriculum Specialist
Florida Department of Education

Capstone
press
Mankato, Minnesota

Capstone Press
151 Good Counsel Drive, P.O. Box 669, Mankato, Minnesota 56002
http://www.capstone-press.com

Library of Congress Cataloging-in-Publication Data
McAuliffe, Emily
   Florida facts and symbols/by Emily McAuliffe.—Rev. and updated ed.
   p. cm.—(The states and their symbols)
   Includes bibliographical references (p. 23) and index.
   Summary: Presents information about the state of Florida, its nickname, motto, and emblems.
   ISBN 0-7368-2239-9 (hardcover)
   1. Emblems, State—Florida—Juvenile literature. [1. Emblems, State—Florida.
2. Florida] I. Title. II. Series: McAuliffe, Emily. States and their symbols.
CR203.F6M38 2003
975.9—dc21   2002154777

Editorial Credits

Christianne C. Jones, update editor; Cara Van Voorst, editor; Kim Covert, additional editing; Linda Clavel, update designer and illustrator; Clay Schotzko/Icon Productions, cover designer; James Franklin, illustrator; Kelly Garvin, update photo researcher; Michelle L. Norstad, photo researcher

Photo Credits

Kevin Barry, 14
Elizabeth DeLaney, 18
Dembinsky Photo Assoc., Inc./Doug Locke, 22 (bottom)
Charles W. Melton, 12
One Mile Up, Inc., 8, 10 (inset)
Marty Saccone and Helen Longest-Slaughter, 22 (top)
Michael P. Turco, 20
Tom & Pat Leeson, cover
Unicorn Stock Photos/Jeff Grenberg, 6, 22 (middle); Andre Jenny, 10; John A. Schakel Jr., 16

1 2 3 4 5 6 08 07 06 05 04 03

Table of Contents

Fast Facts about Florida

Capital: Tallahassee is the capital of Florida.

Largest City: Jacksonville is the largest city in Florida. About 735,600 people live in Jacksonville.

Size: Florida covers 65,758 square miles (170,313 square kilometers). It is the 22nd largest state.

Location: Florida is on the southeast coast of the United States. It is bordered by Alabama and Georgia.

Population: 15,982,378 people live in Florida (2000 U.S. Census Bureau).

Statehood: Florida became the 27th state on March 3, 1845.

Natural Resources: Florida's natural resources include phosphate rock, limestone, clay, and fish.

Manufactured Goods: Florida workers make food, electric equipment, transportation equipment, and machinery.

Crops: Florida farmers grow oranges, grapefruits, and other fruits.

Ponce de Leon discovered Florida on Easter in 1513. De Leon was a Spanish explorer. An explorer travels to discover what a place is like.

There is a Spanish feast on Easter. There are many flowers at this feast. In Spanish, the word Florida means flowers. De Leon named Florida in honor of the Easter flowers.

Florida has many nicknames. People call Florida the Sunshine State. The days are often warm and sunny in Florida.

People also call Florida the Everglades State. The Everglades is a large, swampy area in south Florida. A swamp is a wetland. It has spongy ground and thick plant growth.

People call Florida the Sunshine State.

State Seal and Motto

The state seal is a small picture pressed into wax. Government officials stamp the seal on important papers. The seal makes government papers official.

The state seal is a symbol. A symbol is an object that reminds people of something larger. For example, the U.S. flag reminds people of the United States.

Florida adopted its state seal in 1868. The seal shows rays from the sun and a palm tree. These stand for Florida's warm weather. A Native American woman and a steamboat appear on the seal. Native Americans were the first people to live in Florida. Many steamboats traveled on Florida's rivers in the late 1800s.

Florida's state motto is In God We Trust. A motto is a word or saying. Florida's motto means that people depend on God. The state government adopted the motto in 1868.

Florida adopted its state seal in 1868.

State Capitol and Flag

Tallahassee is the capital of Florida. A capital is the city where government is based.

The capitol is in Tallahassee. Government officials work in this building. Some officials make laws for the state. Others make sure the laws are carried out.

Workers completed the first capitol in 1845. They built a new 22-story capitol in 1977. People call the original building the Old Capitol. The Old Capitol is now a museum. A museum is a building that holds historical objects.

Florida voters chose the state flag in 1900. A large red X appears in the middle of the flag. The state seal covers the center of the X. The rest of the flag is white.

Florida has flown five national flags. Spain, France, and Great Britain have ruled Florida. The flag of the southern states also flew over Florida. This happened during the Civil War (1861-1865). Today, Florida flies the flag of the United States.

Florida's capitol is in Tallahassee. The new capitol is located behind the Old Capitol.

State Bird

The mockingbird is Florida's state bird. It became the state bird in 1910. It is also the state bird of Arkansas, Mississippi, Tennessee, and Texas.

Mockingbirds are about 10 inches (25 centimeters) long. They have gray and white feathers and long tails.

Mockingbirds mock the songs of other birds. Mock means to copy. Mockingbirds can copy the songs of about 40 birds. They can also copy other sounds. They even mock barking dogs.

Mockingbirds build their nests from twigs. They make their nests in bushes or trees. Their nests are cup-shaped. Mockingbirds eat bugs, spiders, and fruits.

Female mockingbirds lay four to five eggs each summer. The eggs are blue-green with brown spots. Mockingbirds are fearless when they guard their young. They attack dogs, cats, and humans that approach mockingbird nests.

Mockingbirds have gray and white feathers.

State Tree

The sabal palm tree is Florida's state tree. State officials adopted it in 1953. Sabal palm trees are common throughout Florida. They can grow in most kinds of soil.

Sabal palms grow up to 80 feet (24 meters) high. Palm trees have tall, straight trunks. There are no branches on the trunks. The trunks reach 18 inches (46 centimeters) across. Many wide, flat leaves grow at the tops of the trees.

There are many uses for sabal palm trees. People plant them to make lawns beautiful. Builders make boat docks from the palm's trunk. The tree's leaves and stems are also useful. People make mats, baskets, and brushes out of the leaves.

Sabal palm trees are common throughout Florida.

State Flower

The orange blossom became Florida's state flower in 1909. A blossom is the flower on a fruit tree or plant. Orange blossoms make seeds. Oranges grow from these seeds.

Orange blossoms bloom from February to April. Bloom means to flower. Each orange blossom has four or five petals. Petals are the colored outer parts of flowers. The orange blossom's petals are white.

Orange blossom petals fall off the trees after blooming. Then oranges start to grow. Florida oranges usually start to ripen in October.

Orange blossoms have a sweet scent. Companies make perfume out of oil from the blossoms. The leaves of the orange tree also have a sweet scent.

Orange blossoms bloom from February to April.

State Animal

The Florida panther is Florida's state animal. Students in Florida chose the panther in 1982.

Florida panthers are large cats. They are about six feet (1.8 meters) long. Males weigh up to 150 pounds (68 kilograms). Panthers have light brown or rusty fur and long tails.

Florida panthers live in trees in the Everglades. They eat white-tailed deer, wild hogs, and raccoons.

The Florida panther is an endangered animal. Endangered means in danger of dying out. Scientists think only 30 to 50 Florida panthers are alive in the wild.

The U.S. government and other groups work to keep panthers safe. They want to increase the number of Florida panthers.

The Florida panther is an endangered animal.

More State Symbols

State Beverage: Orange juice is the state beverage. Florida produces more orange juice than any other state.

State Butterfly: The zebra longwing is the state butterfly. Zebra longwings are black and yellow.

State Reptile: The alligator is Florida's state reptile. Many alligators live in the Everglades.

State Salt Water Mammal: The porpoise is Florida's state salt water mammal. Porpoises can live to be 30 years old.

State Shell: The horse conch is the state shell. The word conch comes from the Greek word for shell. The horse conch is up to 24 inches (61 centimeters) long.

State Soil: Myakka fine sand is the state soil. This white-gray sand is the most common soil in Florida.

State Song: "Old Folks at Home" is the state song. Some people call it "The Swanee River." Stephen C. Foster wrote it in 1851.

The alligator is Florida's state reptile.

Places to Visit

Everglades National Park

Everglades National Park covers more than 1,509,000 acres (610,692 hectares). Many people call the Everglades a "river of grass." Many kinds of wildlife live in the park. The park is home to more than 1,000 alligators. Visitors hike on nature trails, boat, and fish in the park.

The Kennedy Space Center

The Kennedy Space Center is on Florida's eastern coast. Workers built it as a launch area. Launch means to send a rocket into space. Space flights have been launched from this center since 1968. Visitors tour the center. They see the most powerful rocket ever built.

Walt Disney World

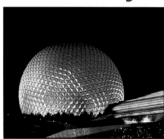

Walt Disney World is a park in Orlando. There are three areas in Walt Disney World. They are the Magic Kingdom, Epcot Center, and Disney-MGM Studios. The Magic Kingdom opened in 1971. It includes rides, shows, shops, and seven make-believe lands.

Words to Know

blossom (BLOSS-uhm)—a flower on a fruit tree or plant
endangered (en-DAYN-jurd)—in danger of dying out
explorer (ek-SPLOR-ur)—a person who travels to discover what a place is like
launch (LAWNCH)—to send a rocket into space
motto (MOT-oh)—a word or saying
petals (PET-uhls)—the colored outer parts of flowers
swamp (SWAHMP)—a wetland with spongy ground and thick plant growth
symbol (SIM-buhl)—an object that reminds people of something larger

Read More

Capstone Press Geography Department. *Florida.* One Nation. Mankato, Minn.: Capstone Press, 2003.

Christian, Sandra J. *Florida.* Land of Liberty. Mankato, Minn.: Capstone Press, 2003.

Heinrichs, Ann. *Florida.* This Land is Your Land. Minneapolis: Compass Point Books, 2002.

Knotts, Bob. *Uniquely Florida.* State Studies. Chicago: Heinemann Library, 2002.

Useful Addresses

Florida Department of State
PL–02, The Capitol
Tallahassee, FL 32399-0250

Florida Office of Tourism
P.O. Box 1100
Tallahassee, FL 32302

Internet Sites

Do you want to find out more about Florida?
Let FactHound, our fact-finding hound dog,
do the research for you.

Here's how:
1) Visit **http://www.facthound.com**
2) Type in the **BOOK ID** number:
   0736822399
3) Click on **FETCH IT**.

FactHound will fetch Internet sites picked by
our editors just for you!

Index